30 POP/ROCK BALLADS
THEN AND NOW

ISBN 1-57560-568-6

Copyright © 2002 by Cherry Lane Music Company
International Copyright Secured   All Rights Reserved

Visit our website at www.cherrylane.com

CONTENTS

Amanda

Words and Music by
Tom Scholz

Babe, to-mor-row's so far a - way. There's some-thin' I just have to say.

I don't think I could hide what I'm feel-in' in-side an -

oth - er day   know-in' I love___ you.

And I,   I'm get - tin' too close___   a -

gain.___   I don't wan - na see   it end.___   If I

tell you to-night,___ will you turn out the light___ and walk a - way   know - in' I love.

You and I,____ I know that we__ can't wait.__ And I swear,____ I swear it's not a lie,____ girl. To-mor-row may be too late.____

You, you and I,— girl, we can share a life— to - geth - er. It's now or nev -

er, and to - mor - row may be too late.——— Oh.———————————

And feel - in' the way— I do,——— I don't wan - na wait my whole life

through——— to say I'm in love with you.

Can't Help Falling in Love

from the Paramount Picture BLUE HAWAII

Words and Music by
George David Weiss, Hugo Peretti
and Luigi Creatore

Fields of Gold

Written and Composed by
G.M. Sumner

Flowing, moderately

You'll re - mem - ber me, when the west wind moves _ up a -
stay with me, will you be my love ___ a -

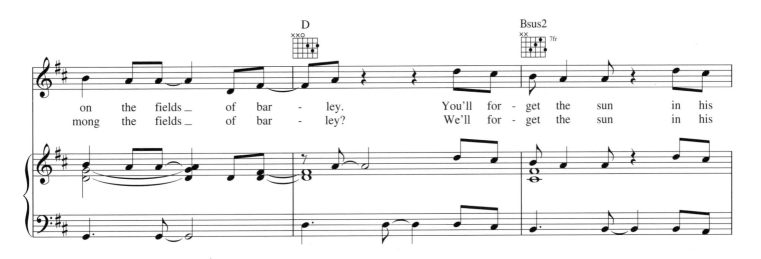

on the fields _ of bar - ley. You'll for - get the sun in his
mong the fields _ of bar - ley? We'll for - get the sun in his

jeal - ous sky   as we walk in   fields __ of gold.
jeal - ous sky   as we lie in   fields __ of gold.

So she
See the

took her love   for to gaze a - while __   up - on the fields __ of bar -
west wind move   like a lov - er so ____   up - on the fields __ of bar -

- ley.   In his arms she fell   as her hair came down   a - mong __
- ley.   Feel her bod - y rise   when you kiss her mouth   a - mong __

Man - y years have passed since those __ sum - mer days a - mong the fields __ of bar - ley. See the
mem - ber me when the __ west wind moves up - on the fields __ of bar - ley. You can

Dog & Butterfly

Words and Music by
Ann Wilson, Nancy Wilson
and Sue Ennis

ing   mak - ing us give in.____   Hearts roll - ing in,____

tak - en back on __ the tide. ____   We're bal-anced to - geth - er;

o - cean up - on __ the sky. _____

D. S. % al Coda ⊕

An -

Feel Like Makin' Love

Words and Music by
Eugene McDaniels

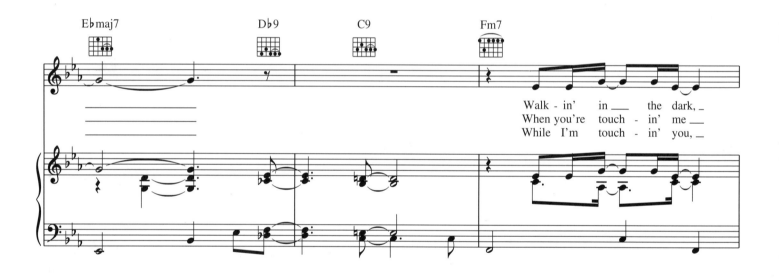

For Always

from the Motion Picture A.I. ARTIFICIAL INTELLIGENCE

Lyric by Cynthia Weil

Music by John Williams

Give Me Forever
(I Do)

Words and Music by
Carter Cathcart, John Tesh,
Juni Morrison and James Ingram

Look - ing out,___ I see,___ and I
With this ring___ I'm bound,___ and I

know   just how   much_____   you're a   part of me.   I
prom - ise that I'll_____   nev - er let you down.—   To

see   you and   I_____   to - geth - er in life,   so there's
fam - 'ly and friends_____   and the Lord_____ up a - bove,   I will

noth - ing I   would - n't do   to make you my___ wife. }
swear I'll be true to you   and give you my___ love. }

Won't you___ give me for - ev - er to___ show

38

From a Distance

Words and Music by
Julie Gold

41

Verse 2:
From a distance, we all have enough,
And no one is in need.
There are no guns, no bombs, no diseases,
No hungry mouths to feed.
From a distance, we are instruments
Marching in a common band;
Playing songs of hope, playing songs of peace,
They're the songs of every man.
(To Bridge:)

Verse 3:
From a distance, you look like my friend
Even though we are at war.
From a distance I just cannot comprehend
What all this fighting is for.
From a distance there is harmony
And it echos through the land.
It's the hope of hopes, it's the love of loves.
It's the heart of every man.

Gold

Words by Nan Knighton

Music by Frank Wildhorn

46

Heaven

Words and Music by
Bryan Adams and Jim Vallance

I Can't Make You Love Me

Words and Music by
Mike Reid and Allen Shamblin

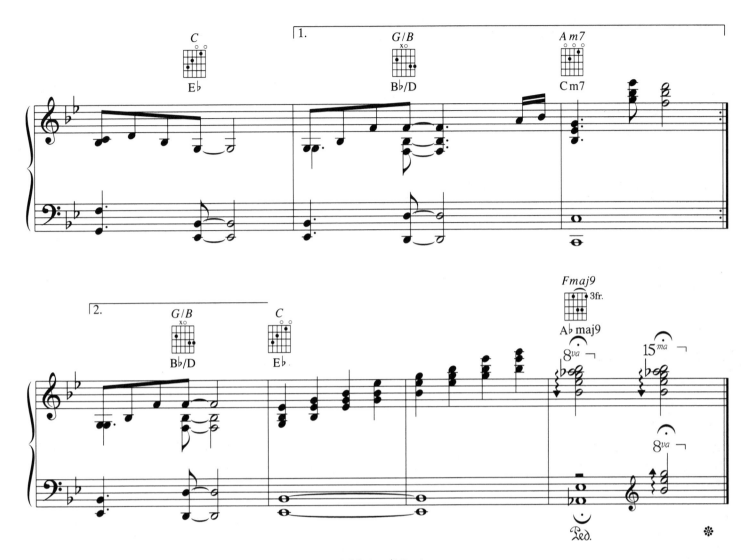

Additional Lyrics

2. I'll close my eyes, then I won't see
   The love you don't feel when you're holdin' me.
   Mornin' will come and I'll do what's right.
   Just give me till then to give up this fight.
   And I will give up this fight. *(To Chorus)*

I Want to Know What Love Is

Words and Music by
Mick Jones

I bet-ter read be-tween the lines, in case I
need it when I'm old - er.

Now, this moun-tain I must climb feels like the world up-on my shoul-
I'm gon-na take a lit-tle time, a lit-tle time to look a-round

64

I Will Come to You

Words and Music by
Isaac Hanson, Taylor Hanson
and Zac Hanson

*Recorded a half step lower.

to you. Some - times when all your dreams may have

seen bet - ter days ___ and you don't know how or why but you've

lost your way, ___ have no fear when your tears are fall - ing.

I will hear your spir - it call - ing, and I swear that I'll be there. Come ___

with me. When the night is dark and storm-y, you won't

have to reach out for me. I will come to you, _ oh, _ I will come _

to you. _ Woh, woh. We all need some-bod-y we can turn

to, oh, woh, _ woh, some-one _ who al-ways _ un-der-stands. _

* From this point till end, recorded a half step higher than written.

Leaving on a Jet Plane

Words and Music by
John Denver

bye.
thing.

But the dawn is break - in', it's ear - ly morn._ The
Ev - 'ry place I go_ I'll think of you._ Ev - 'ry

tax - i's wait - in', he's_ blow - in' his horn._ Al - read - y I'm_ so lone - some I_ could die.
song I sing I'll sing for you._ When I come back_ I'll wear_ your wed - ding ring._

So kiss me_ and smile for me._ Tell me_ that you'll wait for me.

It Is You
(I Have Loved)
from the DreamWorks Motion Picture SHREK

Words and Music by
Dana Glover, Harry Gregson-Williams,
John Powell and Gavin Greenaway

What an un - ex - pect - ed way on this un - ex - pect - ed

day.___ Could it be this is where I ___ be - long?

It is you I ___ have loved all ___ a - long.

There's no more mys - ter - y, it is fi - n'lly clear ___ to

sweet - est _____ de - vo - tion, _____ as I _____

look in - to your per - fect _____ face. _____

There's no more mys - ter - y, it is

fi - n'lly clear _____ to me. You're the home my heart

Missing You

Words and Music by
Joshua P. Thompson, Tim Kelley,
Bob Robinson and Joe Thomas

Never Had a Dream Come True

Words and Music by
Cathy Dennis and Simon Ellis

seems to grow __ with time. _____ There's no use look-ing back or won-der-ing how it

could be __ now or might have been. All this I know but still __ I can't find

ways to let you __ go. I nev-er had a dream come true till the day that

I found _____ you. Ev-en though __ I pre-tend _ that I've moved _ on, you'll

al - ways be ___ my ba - by. I nev - er found the words to

say you're the one I think a - bout ___ each day. And I know no

mat - ter where _ life takes me _ to, a part of me ___ will

al - ways _ be with ___ you, _____ yeah! _

92

love is a strange and __ fun-ny thing. No mat-ter how I try and try I

just can't say good - bye, no, no, no, no! I've nev-er had a

dream come true till the day that I found _____ you. Ev-en though __

I pre-tend __ that I've moved __ on, you'll al-ways be __ my ba - by. I nev-er found the

words to say, you're the one I think a-bout _ each day. And I know no

mat-ter where _ life takes me _ to, a part of me _ will

al-ways _ be. A part of me _ will al-ways _ be with _ you, _

ooh. _

Nights in White Satin

love you,_____ Oh,_____ how I love__ you._____

love__ you._____

Oh,_how I love

you._____

Not a Day Goes By

Words and Music by
Steve Diamond and Maribeth Derry

* Recorded a half step lower.

99

mem - 'ry of you ____ I car - ry in ___ my soul. ___
still a - maz - es me that I lie here in ___ the dark, ___

I wrap it close a - round _ me ____ when the nights get cold. ___
wish - in' you were next __ to __ me with your head a - gainst my heart. __

If you asked me how I'm do - in', I'd say, "Just fine." __

But the truth is, ba - by, ____ if you could read __ my mind, __ not a

November Rain

Words and Music by
W. Axl Rose

* Recorded a half step lower

ken heart,— would-n't time— be out— to charm— you? Woh._____

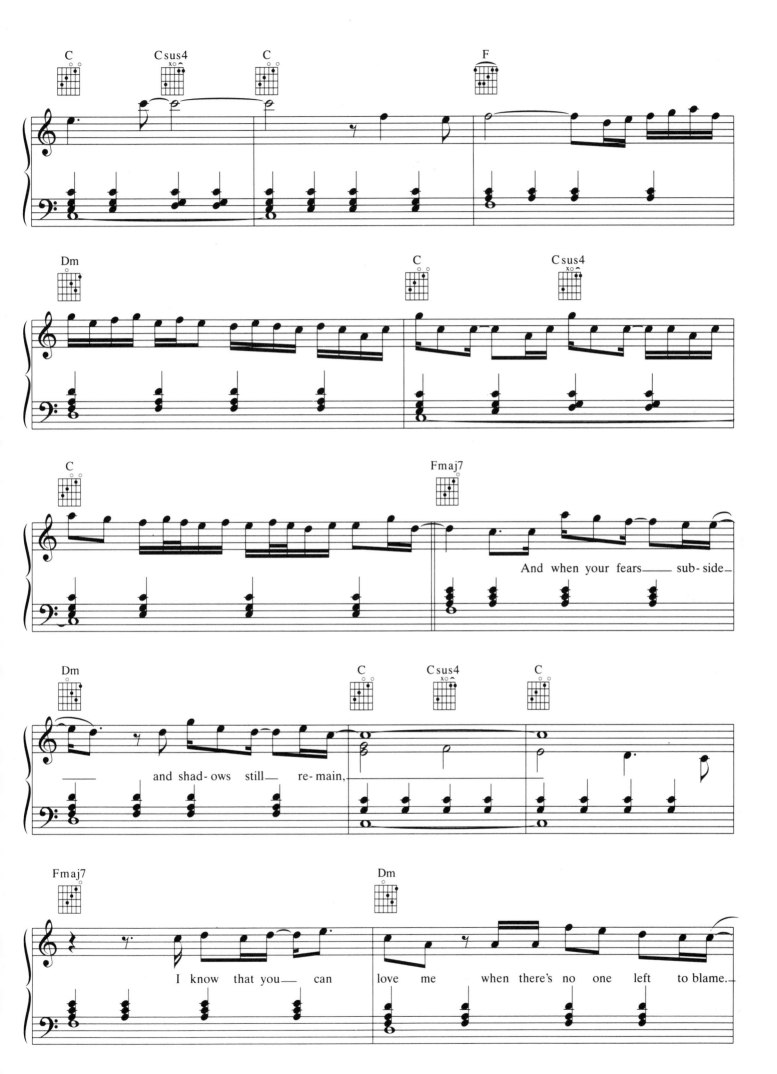

And when your fears——— sub-side

———— and shad-ows still——— re-main,

I know that you—— can love me when there's no one left to blame.

So nev - er mind___ the dark-ness. We still can find a- way.___ Noth-in' lasts___ for - ev - er, e - ven cold No - vem - ber rain.___

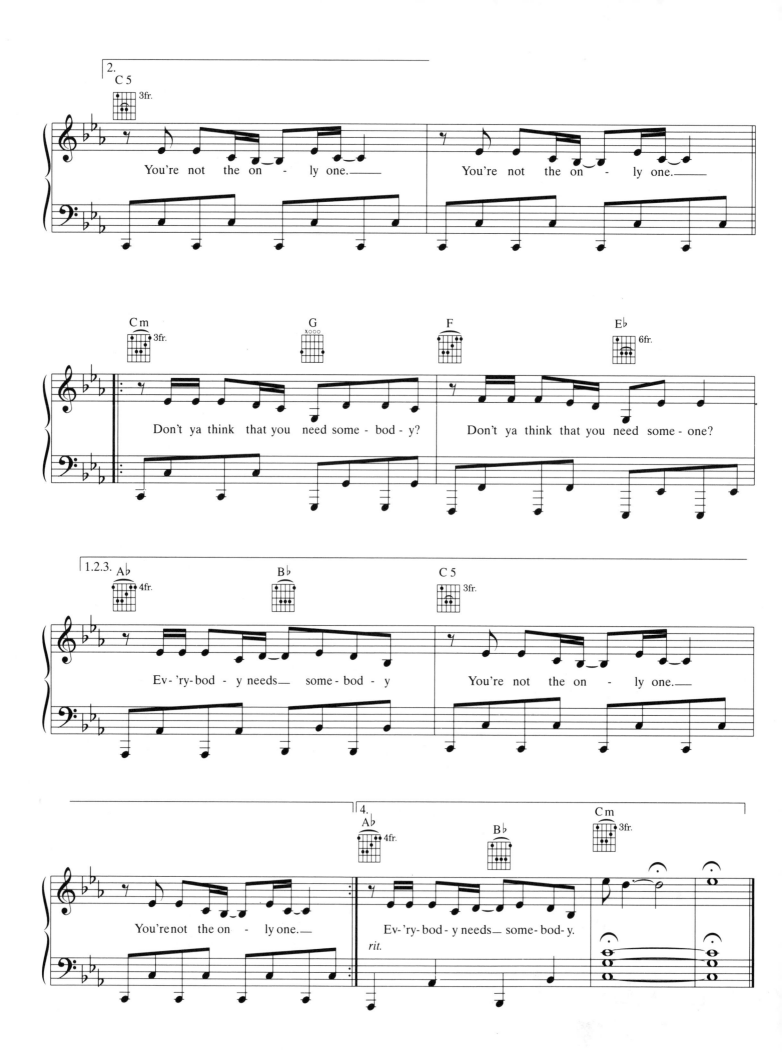

A Whiter Shade of Pale

Words and Music by
Keith Reid and Gary Brooker

We skipped the light___ fan - dan - go,_____ turned cart - wheels 'cross the
She said, "I'm home___ on shore leave,"_____ though in truth we___ were at
She said, "There is___ no rea - son,_____ and the truth is___ plain to

floor;___ I was feel - ing kind of sea - sick,
sea;___ So I took her by the look - ing glass
see,"___ But I wan - dered through my play - ing cards

Save the Best for Last

Words and Music by
Phil Galdston, Jon Lind
and Wendy Waldman

Just when I thought ____ our chance ____ had passed, ____ you go and save ____ the best ____ for last. ____

All of the nights ____

Smile

Words and Music by
Chris Lindsey and Keith Follesé

I could hold on ____ a lit-tle tight-er, I ____ know. ____ But when you
Give me a chance to bow out ____ grace-ful - - ly, ____

love some - one, ____ you got-ta let 'em go. ____ So I'm gon-na smile, _
'cause that's how I want you to re-mem-ber me. _____ I'm gon-na smile, _

'cause I wan-na make _ you hap-py.

Laugh, so ____ you can't see me cry. ____ I'm gon-na

Superman

(It's Not Easy)

Words and Music by
John Ondrasik

I'm just out ___ to find ___ the bet - ter part ___ of me. ___

___ I'm more than a bird. ___ I'm more than a plane. ___ I'm more than some

pret - ty face ___ be - side a train. And it's not eas - y to be ___

___ me.   I

129

sleep sound ____ to-night. ____ I'm not cra - zy ____

or - an - y - thing. ____ I can't stand ____ to fly. ____

I'm not that ____ na - ive. ____

Men weren't meant ____ to ride ____ with ____ clouds ____ be - tween ____ their knees. ____

ooh,   ooh, ____   ooh. ____   It's not eas-

-y ____   to be ____   me.

Superstar

Words and Music by
Leon Russell and Bonnie Sheridan

This Masquerade

Words and Music by
Leon Russell

Guitar Solo

*Guitar solo sounds 8va
lower than written.

142

143

This Woman Needs

Words and Music by Kristyn Osborn,
Bonnie Baker and Connie Harrington

*Sing bkgd. vocal 2nd time only.

144

lay by my side _____ and I'll tell you, I'll

tell you. This wom-an tell you what this ___ wom-an ____

needs. _____

Oh, _____ what this ___ wom-an needs ____ is some-where to

Trying

Words and Music by
Jason Wade and Ron Aniello

Could you let down your hair, __ be trans - par - ent for a while, just a

lit - tle while, to see if you're __ hu - man af - ter all?

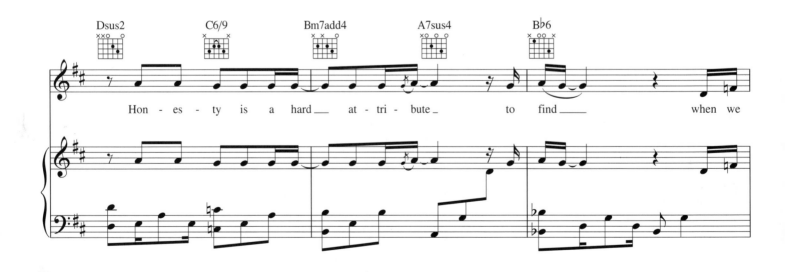

Hon - es - ty is a hard __ at - tri - bute __ to find __ when we

Waiting for a Girl Like You

Words and Music by
Mick Jones and Lou Gramm

me if I'm coming on too strong? This heart of mine has been hurt before. This time I wanna be sure. I've been waiting for a girl like you to come into my life. I've been waiting for a girl like you, a

160

You're Still a Young Man

Words and Music by
Stephen Kupka and Emilio Castillo

Down on my knees,____
Back once a - gain,____
time.____ The dam - age is done.____

oh,____
ooh,____
You'll____

heart____
just beg - gin'
see____

in hand,____
you please.____
that your were wrong.____

I was ac - cused____
Dar - ling,
You'll wake up won - der - ing just____

of be - ing
think twice____
how well I've

too

a - bout

young.____
me,____
done.____

But I'm
'cause I'm
Well, I've

not so young.____
not so bad.____
done all right.____

More Great Piano/Vocal Books from Cherry Lane

For a complete listing of Cherry Lane titles available, including contents listings, please visit our web site at
www.cherrylane.com

02500343	Almost Famous	$14.95
02501801	Amistad	$14.95
02502171	The Best of Boston	$17.95
02500144	Mary Chapin Carpenter – Party Doll and Other Favorites	$16.95
02502163	Mary Chapin Carpenter – Stones in the Road	$17.95
02502165	John Denver Anthology – Revised	$22.95
02502227	John Denver – A Celebration of Life	$14.95
02500002	John Denver Christmas	$14.95
02502166	John Denver's Greatest Hits	$17.95
02502151	John Denver – A Legacy in Song (Softcover)	$24.95
02502152	John Denver – A Legacy in Song (Hardcover)	$34.95
02500326	John Denver – The Wildlife Concert	$17.95
02509922	The Songs of Bob Dylan	$29.95
02500396	Linda Eder – Christmas Stays the Same	$17.95
02500175	Linda Eder – It's No Secret Anymore	$14.95
02502209	Linda Eder – It's Time	$17.95
02509912	Erroll Garner Songbook, Vol. 1	$17.95
02500270	Gilbert & Sullivan for Easy Piano	$12.95
02500318	Gladiator	$12.95
02500273	Gold & Glory: The Road to El Dorado	$16.95
02502126	Best of Guns N' Roses	$17.95
02502072	Guns N' Roses – Selections from Use Your Illusion I and II	$17.95
02500014	Sir Roland Hanna Collection	$19.95
02500352	Hanson – This Time Around	$16.95
02502134	Best of Lenny Kravitz	$12.95
02500012	Lenny Kravitz – 5	$16.95
02500381	Lenny Kravitz – Greatest Hits	$14.95
02500003	Dave Matthews Band – Before These Crowded Streets	$17.95
02502199	Dave Matthews Band – Crash	$17.95
02502192	Dave Matthews Band – Under the Table and Dreaming	$17.95
02500081	Natalie Merchant – Ophelia	$14.95
02500423	Natalie Merchant – Tigerlily	$14.95
02502204	The Best of Metallica	$17.95
02500407	O-Town	$14.95
02500010	Tom Paxton – The Honor of Your Company	$17.95
02507962	Peter, Paul & Mary – Holiday Concert	$17.95
02500145	Pokemon 2.B.A. Master	$12.95
02500026	The Prince of Egypt	$16.95
02502189	The Bonnie Raitt Collection	$22.95

02502230	Bonnie Raitt – Fundamental	$17.95
02502139	Bonnie Raitt – Longing in Their Hearts	$16.95
02502088	Bonnie Raitt – Luck of the Draw	$14.95
02507958	Bonnie Raitt – Nick of Time	$14.95
02502190	Bonnie Raitt – Road Tested	$24.95
02502218	Kenny Rogers – The Gift	$16.95
02500072	Saving Private Ryan	$14.95
02500197	SHeDAISY – The Whole SHeBANG	$14.95
02500414	SHREK	$14.95
02500166	Steely Dan – Anthology	$17.95
02500284	Steely Dan – Two Against Nature	$14.95
02500165	Best of Steely Dan	$14.95
02502132	Barbra Streisand – Back to Broadway	$19.95
02507969	Barbra Streisand – A Collection: Greatest Hits and More	$17.95
02502164	Barbra Streisand – The Concert	$22.95
02502228	Barbra Streisand – Higher Ground	$16.95
02500196	Barbra Streisand – A Love Like Ours	$16.95
02500280	Barbra Streisand – Timeless	$22.95
02503617	John Tesh – Avalon	$15.95
02502178	The John Tesh Collection	$17.95
02503623	John Tesh – A Family Christmas	$15.95
02505511	John Tesh – Favorites for Easy Piano	$12.95
02503630	John Tesh – Grand Passion	$16.95
02500124	John Tesh – One World	$14.95
02500307	John Tesh – Pure Movies 2	$16.95
02502175	Tower of Power – Silver Anniversary	$17.95
02502198	The "Weird Al" Yankovic Anthology	$17.95
02502217	Trisha Yearwood – A Collection of Hits	$16.95
02500334	Maury Yeston – December Songs	$17.95
02502225	The Maury Yeston Songbook	$19.95

See your local music dealer or contact:

CHERRY LANE MUSIC COMPANY
6 East 32nd Street, New York, NY 10016

EXCLUSIVELY DISTRIBUTED BY

HAL•LEONARD CORPORATION
7777 W. BLUEMOUND RD. P.O. BOX 13819 MILWAUKEE, WI 53213

Prices, contents and availability subject to change without notice.

0402